All patterns have been independently tested for accuracy.

TABLE OF CONTENTS

Layla Vest 4

Snowflake Poncho 9

Eiffel Tower Tween Girls' Sweater 15

Girls' Skull Poncho 21

CROCHET ABBREVIATIONS 24

Copyright © 2017 Lisa Ferrel, My Fingers Fly
No pattern or photograph may be reproduced or distributed - mechanically, electronically, or by any other means, including photocopying, without written permission of Lisa Ferrel. If purchasing this pattern to offer finished products for commercial sale, it would be greatly appreciated if you credit the design to My Fingers Fly (www.myfingersfly.com) in your listing. Not intended for bulk commercial sale.

Layla Vest

Girls' size 10 [12, 14]

Materials:
I Love This Cotton 3 [3, 4] skeins
Size G (4.00 mm) crochet hook
Yarn needle

Cluster st: *yo, insert hook, pull through, yo, pull through 2 loops* 3 times, yo and pull through all loops.
Sideways cluster st: ch 3 off top of cluster st, *yo, insert hook, pull through, yo, pull through 2 loops* 2 times, yo and pull through all loops.

See YouTube for video explaining cluster stitch - https://youtu.be/_hlE1AbRyUE

BACK:
Row 1: Ch 61 [65, 69], dc in 4th ch and each ch across (59 [63, 67] dc).
Row 2: Ch 4 (counts as first dc and ch-1), dc in third st, *ch 1, sk 1 st, dc next st.* Repeat across. Turn. Row 3: Ch 3 (counts as first dc), sk 1 st, dc in each st and each ch-1 sp. Dc in third ch of ch-4. Turn. Row 4: Ch 3 [3, 4] (counts as first dc [and ch-1]), sk 1st st, *cluster next st, ch 3 (counts as 1st dc of cluster), 2 dc tog to complete side cluster, sk 2 sts,* repeat across. Sk 1 [0, 1] st, dc in top of ch-3. Turn. Row 5: Ch 3 (counts as 1st dc), *cluster st in top of cluster, ch 2,* repeat across. Dc in top of ch-3 [size 14 – dc in 3rd and 4th chs of ch-4). Turn. (59 [63, 67] dc)
Row 6: Ch 3 (counts as 1st dc), sk 1st dc, *dc in top of cluster, 2 dc in ch-2 sp,* repeat across. Dc in top of ch-3. Turn.
Rows 7-11: Repeat Rows 2-6.
Rows 12-13 [12-13, 17-18]: Repeat Rows 2-3. Row 14 [14, 19]: Sl st first 7 sts, ch 3, Repeat row of cluster pattern. Do not work last 5 sts or top of ch-3.
(17 V clusters)
Row 15 [15, 20]: Repeat Row 5.
Row 16 [16, 21]: Repeat Row 6.
Rows 17-21 [17-21, 22-26]: Repeat Rows 2-6.
Rows 22-23 [22-23, 27-28]: Repeat Rows 2-3.
Row 24 [24, 29]: Sl st in 1st 5 sts, ch 4,* sk next st, dc in next st,* repeat across leaving last 5 sts unworked. Turn.
Row 25 [25, 30]: Ch 1, Sl st in first 5 sts, ch 3, *dc in ch-1 sp, dc in dc,* Repeat across. Leave last ch-1 sp, last dc, and ch-4 sp unworked.

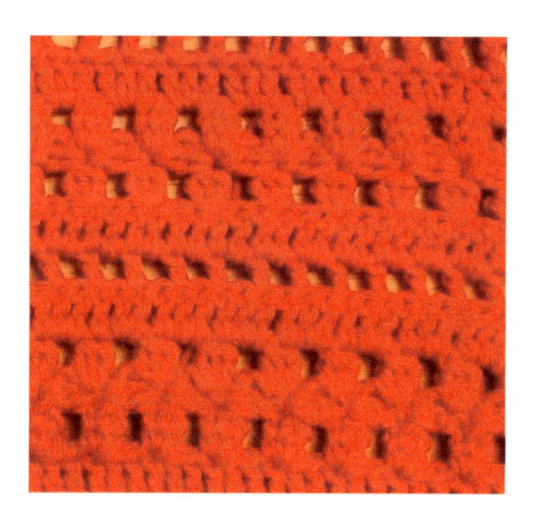

http://www.myfingersfly.com

FRONT LEFT:
Row 1: Ch 32 [35, 38], dc in 4th ch and each ch across (30 [33, 36] dc).
Row 2: Ch 4 (counts as first dc and ch-1), dc in third st, *ch 1, sk 1 st, dc next st.* Repeat across. Turn. Row 3: Ch 3 (counts as first dc), sk 1 st, dc in each st and each ch-1 sp. Dc in third ch of ch-4. Turn. Row 4: Ch 3 [3, 4] (counts as first dc [and ch-1]), sk 1st st, *cluster next st, ch 3 (counts as 1st dc of cluster), 2 dc tog to complete side cluster, sk 2 sts,* repeat across. Sk 1 [0, 1] st, dc in top of ch-3. Turn. Row 5: Ch 3 (counts as 1st dc), *cluster st in top of cluster, ch 2,* repeat across. Dc in top of ch-3 [size 14 – dc in 3rd and 4th chs of ch-4). Turn Row 6: Ch 3 (counts as 1st dc), sk 1st dc, *dc in top of cluster, 2 dc in ch-2 sp,* repeat across. Dc in top of ch-3. Turn.
Rows 7-11: Repeat Rows 2-6.
Rows 12-13 [12-13, 17-18]: Repeat Rows 2-3.
Row 14 [14, 19]: Sl st in first 7 sts, ch 3, sk 1st st, *cluster next st, ch 3 (counts as 1st dc of cluster), 2 dc tog to complete side cluster, sk 2 sts,* repeat across. Sk 1 [0, 1] st, dc in top of ch-3. Turn.
Row 15 [15, 20]: Repeat Row 5.
Row 16 [16, 21]: Repeat Row 6.
Rows 17-18 [17-18, 22-23]: Repeat Rows 2-3. Row 19 [19, 24]: Work in cluster pattern for 8 [8, 9] vertical clusters, dc in next st. Leave remaining 3 sts unworked.
Row 20 [20, 25]: Repeat Row 5.
Row 21 [21, 26]: Repeat Row 6.
Row 22 [22, 27]: Sl st in 1st 3 sts, ch 4, *dc, skip 1 st, ch 1,* repeat.
Row 23 [23, 28]: Dc in each ch and each dc across. Row 24 [24, 29]: Sl st in 1st 5 sts, ch 4,* sk next st, dc in next st,* repeat across leaving last 5 sts unworked. Turn.
Row 25 [25, 30]: Ch 1, Sl st in first 5 sts, ch 3, *dc in ch-1 sp, dc in dc,* Repeat across. Leave last ch-1 sp, last dc, and ch-4 sp unworked.

FRONT RIGHT:
Row 1: Ch 32 [35, 38], dc in 4th ch and each ch across (30 [33, 36] dc).
Row 2: Ch 4 (counts as first dc and ch-1), dc in third st, *ch 1, sk 1 st, dc next st.* Repeat across. Turn. Row 3: Ch 3 (counts as first dc), sk 1 st, dc in each st and each ch-1 sp. Dc in third ch of ch-4. Turn. Row 4: Ch 3 [3, 4] (counts as first dc [and ch-1]), sk 1st st, *cluster next st, ch 3 (counts as 1st dc of cluster), 2 dc tog to complete side cluster, sk 2 sts,* repeat across. Sk 1 [0, 1] st, dc in top of ch-3. Turn. Row 5: Ch 3 (counts as 1st dc), *cluster st in top of cluster, ch 2,* repeat across. Dc in top of ch-3 [size 14 – dc in 3rd and 4th chs of ch-4). Turn Row 6: Ch 3 (counts as 1st dc), sk 1st dc, *dc in top of cluster, 2 dc in ch-2 sp,* repeat across. Dc in top of ch-3. Turn.
Rows 7-11: Repeat Rows 2-6.
Rows 12-13 [12-13, 17-18]: Repeat Rows 2-3.
Row 14 [14, 19]: Sl st in first 7 sts, ch 3, sk 1st st, *cluster next st, ch 3 (counts as 1st dc of cluster), 2 dc tog to complete side cluster, sk 2 sts,* repeat across. Sk 1 [0, 1] st, dc in top of ch-3. Turn.
Row 15 [15, 20]: Repeat Row 5.
Row 16 [16, 21]: Repeat Row 6.
Rows 17-18 [17-18, 22-23]: Repeat Rows 2-3. Row 19 [19, 24]: Sl st in

first 3 sts, work in cluster pattern for 9 [9, 10] vertical clusters.
Row 20 [20, 25]: Repeat Row 5.
Row 21 [21, 26]: Repeat Row 6.
Row 22 [22, 27]: *Dc, skip 1 st, ch 1,* repeat, leaving last 3 sts unworked. .
Row 23 [23, 28]: Dc in each ch and each dc across. Row 24 [24, 29]: Sl st in 1st 5 sts, ch 4,* sk next st, dc in next st,* repeat across leaving last 5 sts unworked. Turn.
Row 25 [25, 30]: Ch 1, Sl st in first 5 sts, ch 3, *dc in ch-1 sp, dc in dc,* Repeat across. Leave last ch-1 sp, last dc, and ch-4 sp unworked.

ASSEMBLY:
With right sides together, stitch front left and front right to back at shoulders. Stitch side seams.

With right side facing, join yarn at front left in unused loop of starting ch. Sc across bottom with 2 sc in last loop. Turn to work up right side with 2 sc in the side of each dc. Lay the work on a flat surface to ensure edging lays even. Continue to work 1 sc in each st around neck. Work left side edging same as right side. Count sts to ensure right and left sides are even. Join with sl st in 1st sc.

FRINGE:
Cut lengths of yarn 16-24" long. Pull through sc edging at bottom of vest – 1 strand in each sc or 2 strands every other sc. If desired, tie beads onto fringe.

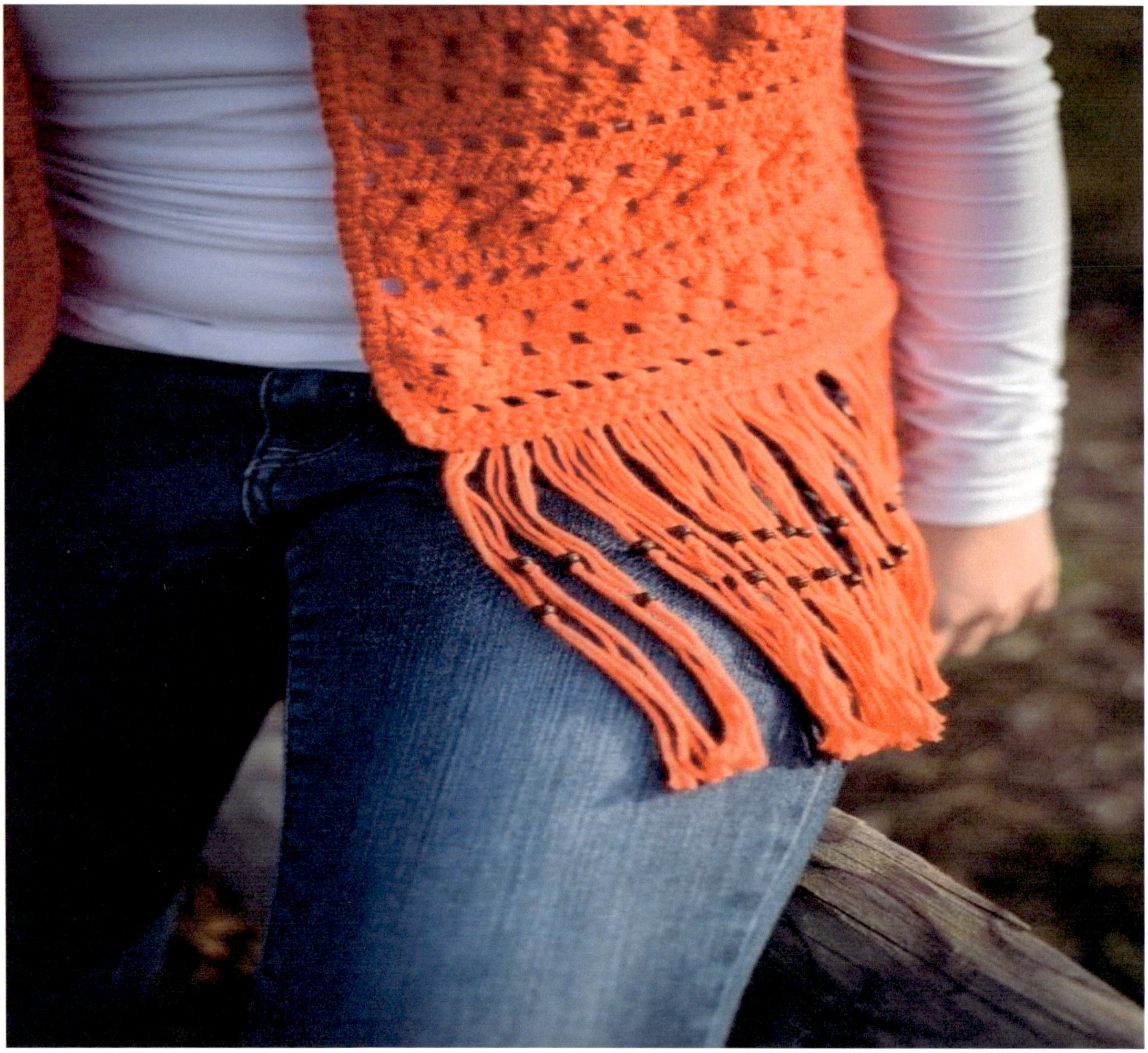

Snowflake Poncho
Girls' size 8/10,
Girls' size 12/14, and Ladies' size Medium

Materials:

2 [3, 3] skeins Baby Bee Sweet Delight Pomp – Blue Boy/color 250
1 skein Baby Bee Sweet Delight – Angel/color 210
Size C (2.75 mm) crochet hook for girls' 8/10
Size F (3.75 mm) crochet hook for girls' 12/14
Size G (4.0 mm) crochet hook for ladies' medium

Gauge:
With C hook, hexagon measures 4 ¾"
With F hook, hexagon measures 5 ½"
With G hook, hexagon measures 6"

Snowflake Square (Make 28; for extra length make 34):

Rnd 1: With white yarn, ch 2, work 6 sc in 2nd ch. Join. (Do not turn.)

Rnd 2: Ch 4 (counts as 1st dc and ch 1), dc in 1st stitch, (dc, ch 1, dc) 5 times. Join with slip stitch in 3rd ch of ch-4.

Rnd 3: Sl st in ch-1 space. Ch 3 (counts ad dc) dc, ch1, 2 dc in ch-1 space, ch 1 (2 dc, ch 1, 2 dc, ch 1) in next ch-1 space 5 times. Join with sl st in top of ch-3.

Rnd 4: Ch 3 (counts as 1st dc) dc in next dc, work tr, ch 8, sl st in 1st ch, tr in ch-1 space, dc in each of next 2 dc, ch 2. *Dc in each of next 2 dc (tr, ch 8, sl st in 1 st, tr) in ch-1 space, dc in next 2 dc, ch 2, repeat from * around. Join with sl st in top of ch-3. End off white.

Rnd 5: Join blue, *sc in ch-8 space, ch 5, dc in ch-2 space, ch 5, repeat from * around. Join with sl st in top of 1st sc.

Rnd 6: (Ch 3, 2 dc, ch1, 3 dc) in sc, 3 dc in 3rd ch of ch-5 space (cluster made), 3 dc in next dc, 3 dc in 3rd ch of ch-5 space, *(3 dc, ch 1, 3 dc) in sc, 3 dc in 3rd ch of ch-5, 3 dc in next dc, 3 dc in 3rd ch of ch-5, repeat from * around. Join with sl st in top ch of ch-3.

Rnd 7: Sl st across dc, sl st into ch-1 space, (ch 3, 2 dc, ch 1, 3 dc) in ch-1 space, 3 dc in space between clusters 4 times, *(3 dc, ch 1, 3 dc) in ch-1 space, 3 dc in space between clusters 4 times, repeat from *.

Join with sl st in 3rd ch of ch-3. Fasten off blue, leaving a 12" length for sewing.

If you are using E hook, square will measure approximately 4-5/8".

If you are using G hook, square will measure approximately 5-1/8".

Sew your squares together in rows, staggering them to fit the hexagons together.   Row 1 – 3 squares

Row 2 – 4 squares

Row 3 – 5 squares

Row 4 - 2 squares, then skip space of 2 squares, then 2 more squares (this makes the neck opening).

Row 5: 5 squares

Row 6 - 4 squares

Row 7 -3 squares

For extra length, make 32 squares and sew together in 11 rows:
Row 1 - 1 square
Row 2 - 2 squares
Row 3 - 3 squares
Row 4 - 4 squares
Row 5 – 5 squares
Row 6 - 2 squares, then skip space of 2 squares, then 2 more squares (this makes the neck opening).
Row 7 - 5 squares
Row 8 - 4 squares
Row 9 - 3 squares
Row 10 – 2 squares
Row 11 – 1 square

Neck Edging:

The neck opening as shown in the above photo has a point at the center in both the front and back. Rnd 1: With right side facing, attach blue yarn at 1st stitch of center neck square. Ch 2 (does not count as dc), dec, dc in next 16 dc, sk ch 1 space, dc in next 16 st, dec in last 2 dc of square, dec 1st 2 stitches of next square, *dc in next 14 dc, dec twice, repeat from *. Join. Do not turn.

Rnd 2: Ch 2 (does not count as dc) dec, *dc 30, dec, dec, (12 dc, dec twice) 3 times, repeat from *.

Bottom Edging:

Rnd 1: With right side facing, attach blue yarn at 1st stitch of any square. Ch 2 (does not count as dc), dc in same space, dc in next 17 dc, sk ch 1 space, dc in next 17 st, dec between last dc of this square and 1st dc of next square, *dc in next space, dc in next 17 dc, sk ch 1, dc in next 17 st, dec between last dc of this square and 1st dc of next square, repeat from *.

Fringe: cut 10" lengths of yarn, double 2 pieces at a time and pull through sts of edging.

Approximate finished measurements (not including fringe):

Size 8/10 (C hook) — Neckline to bottom – 15"
Width across shoulders - 31.5"

Size 12/14 (F hook) — Neckline to bottom – 16.5"
Width across shoulders – 35"

Size Ladies' M with 32 hexagons (G hook) — Neckline to bottom – 24"
Width across shoulders – 39"

http://www.myfingersfly.com

Eiffel Tower Tween Girls' Sweater

Girls' Size 10, 12, 14

Materials:
Lion Pound of Love worsted weight yarn
    16 [18, 20] oz. Pastel Pink (MC)
        2 oz. Black
Size G (4.00 mm) crochet hook
Yarn needle

Gauge (G hook) 4 dc = 1", 2 rows dc = 1"

Finished chest measurement: 29" [31", 33"]
Length: 26" [28", 30"]

BACK:
Row 1: With MC yarn and G hook, ch 54 [58, 62]. Dc in 4th ch from hook and each remaining ch (52 [56, 60] dc including ch-3). Row 2: Ch 3 (counts as dc), turn, Skip 1st dc, dc in each dc across.
Repeat Row 2 until back measures 4" [5", 6"].
Next Row: Ch 3, turn, skip 1st st. Dc in each of the next 15 [17, 19] sts. Begin Row 1 of chart. Dc in remaining 16 [18, 20] sts.

Continue working chart in center 20 sts until back measures 14" [15", 16"]. Next Row: Still working according to chart, sl st in 1st 6 sts, ch 3, dc across leaving last 4 sts and ch-3 unworked (43 [47, 51] dc).
Armhole shaping:
Next Row: Ch 3, sk 1st dc, dc 1st 2 sts tog (dec made), dc across. Do not work dc into ch-3 (dec made).
Repeat this row once more (39 [43, 47] dc).
Continue working even in dc until back measures 21" [23", 25"].
Shoulder shaping:
Next Row: Sl st in 1st 4 sts, ch 3, dc across. Do not work last 2 dc or ch-3. Repeat this row once. Fasten off.

Row	1	2	3	4	5	6	7	8	9	10	11	12	13	14	15	16	17	18	19	20
29											X									
28										X	X									
27										X	X									
26										X	X									
25										X	X									
24										X	X									
23										X	X									
22										X	X									
21									X	X	X	X								
20									X	X	X	X								
19									X			X								
18									X			X								
17									X			X								
16							X	X	X	X	X	X								
15							X					X								
14							X	X	X	X	X	X								
13							X	X	X	X	X	X								
12						X	X	X			X	X	X							
11						X	X				X	X								
10					X	X	X	X	X	X	X	X	X	X						
9					X									X						
8					X	X	X	X	X	X	X	X	X	X						
7					X	X	X	X	X	X	X	X	X	X						
6				X	X	X								X	X	X				
5			X	X	X									X	X	X				
4		X	X	X										X	X	X				
3	X	X	X	X										X	X	X	X			
2	X	X	X	X										X	X	X	X			
1	X	X	X	X	X	X								X	X	X	X	X	X	X

RIGHT FRONT:

Row 1: With MC, ch 28 [30, 32]. Dc in 4th ch from hook and each remaining ch (26 [28, 30] dc including ch-3).

Row 2: Sk 1st st, dc across and in ch-3. Ch 3, turn.

Repeat Row 2 until front measures 14" [15", 16"].

Armhole shaping:

Next Row: Sl st in 1st 6 sts, ch 3, dc across (21 [23, 25] dc).

Next Row: Ch 3, turn. Dc in each dc across. Do not dc in ch-3 (dec made).

Next Row: Ch 3, turn. Dc 1st 2 sts tog. Dc across including ch-3 (19 [21, 23] dc).

Neckline shaping:

Next Row: Ch 3, turn, dc across including ch-3.

Next Row: Ch 3, turn. Dc across. Do not dc in ch-3.

Repeat last 2 rows until front measures 2 rows less than back.

Shoulder shaping:

Next Row: Ch 3, turn, dc across. Do not work last 2 dc or ch-3.

Next Row: Sl st in 1st 4 dc, ch 3, dc across. Fasten off.

LEFT FRONT:

Row 1: With MC, ch 28 [30, 32]. Dc in 4th ch from hook and each remaining ch (26 [28, 30] dc including ch-3).

Row 2: Sk 1st st, dc across and in ch-3. Ch 3, turn.

Repeat Row 2 until front measures 14" [15", 16"].

Armhole shaping:

Next Row: ch 3, dc across. Do not dc in last 4 sts or ch-3 (21 [23, 25] dc).

Next Row: Ch 3, turn. Dc 1st 2 sts tog. Dc across including ch-3 (19 [21, 23] dc). Next Row: Ch 3, turn. Dc in each dc across. Do not dc in ch-3 (dec made).

Neckline shaping:

Next Row: Ch 3, turn, dc across including ch-3.

Next Row: Ch 3, turn. Dc 1st 2 sts tog, dc in ch-3.

Repeat last 2 rows until front measures 2 rows less than back.

Shoulder shaping:

Next Row: Sl st in 1st 4 dc, ch 3, dc across. Next Row: Ch 3, turn, dc across. Do not work last 2 dc or ch-3. Fasten off.

SLEEVES (Make 2):
Row 1: With MC, ch 42, dc in 4th ch from hook and in each remaining ch (40 dc including ch-3).
Rows 2-4: Ch 3, turn, sk 1st dc, dc in remaining sts and in top of ch-3 (40 dc).
Row 5: Ch 3, turn, dc in 1st st (inc made), dc across, 2 dc in last dc (inc made), dc in top of ch-3 (42 dc).
Repeat Rows 2-5 1 [1, 2] times (42 [42, 44] dc).
Repeat Row 2 until sleeve measures 7" [7.5", 8"].
Next Row: Sl st in 1st 6 sts, ch 3, dc across. Do not work last 4 dc or ch-3.
Next Row: Ch 3, turn, sk 1st dc, dc across. Do not dc in ch-3 (dec made).
Repeat last row until sleeve measures 12" [12.5", 13"]/

ASSEMBLY:
With right sides together, sew front left and front right to back at shoulder seams. Sew sleeves to body matching center top of sleeve with shoulder seem. Sew underarms together and sew front to back at sides.

EDGING AND RUFFLE:
Rnd 1: With right side facing, attach MC yarn to bottom corner. Ch 1, sc up front with approximately 2 sc per dc. Lay flat on table as you go to make sure edging will lay flat. Continue in sc around collar, back down the other side, and across the bottom of the sweater, working 2 sc in each corner. Join with sl st in beginning sc.
Rnd 2: Ch 3, dc in same st, 2 dc in each st around. Join with sl st in top of ch-3.
Rnd 3: Ch 3, dc in each dc around. Join with sl st in top of ch-3.
Rnds 4-5: Repeat Rnd 3. Fasten off MC.
Rnd 6: Attach black yarn, sc in each st around. Join. Fasten off black.

SLEEVE RUFFLE:
Rnd 1: With right side facing, attach MC yarn to sleeve at seam. Ch 3, dc in same st, 2 dc in each st around. Join with sl st in top of ch-3.
Rnd 2: Ch 3, dc in each dc around. Join with sl st in top of ch-3.
Rnds 3-4: Repeat Rnd 2. Fasten off MC.
Rnd 5: Attach black yarn, sc in each st around. Join. Fasten off black.
Weave in all ends. Press and block sweater. Press ruffle to the outside along right and left front and collar.

Girls' Skull Poncho

Materials:
I Love This Yarn sport weight yarn –
    Black – 2 [2, 3] skeins
Ombre – 2 [2, 3] skeins
Size G (4.00 mm) crochet hook
Yarn needle

Sizes	Small (4/6)	Medium (8/10)	Large (12/14)
Neckline to hem (not including fringe)	15"	20"	25"
Neck opening (circumference)	24"	25.5"	27"
Laying flat at widest point	24"	28"	32"

Gauge:
5 dc = 1".
Skull motif measures 1-3/4 wide x 2" tall

INSTRUCTIONS:
Make 2 (1 front & 1 back)
With black yarn, ch 110 [126, 142].
Row 1: Dc in 4th ch from hook and each ch across (108 [124, 140 dc including beginning ch-3).
Row 2: Ch 3 (counts as 1st dc), dc across. End black.
Row 3: Join ombre yarn, ch 3 (counts as 1st dc), dc in next 3 dc, *ch 4, skip 4 dc, dc in next 4 dc*, repeat across.
Row 4: Ch 3, dc in next 3 dc, ch 2, *2 dc in next st, dc in each of next 2 st, 2 dc in next st, ch 2* repeat across, dc in last 4 st.
Row 5: Ch 3, dc in next 3 dc, ch 1, *2 dc in next st, ch 1, skip 1 st (eye socket), dc in each of next 2 st, ch 1, skip 1 st, 2 dc in next st, ch 1* repeat across, dc in last 4 st.
Row 6: Ch 3, dc in next 3 dc, ch 1, *dec in first 2 st, dc in ch-1 space, dc in each of next 2 st, dc in ch-1 space, dec in next 2 st, ch 1* repeat across, dc in last 4 st. Fasten off ombre. (12 [14, 16] skulls)
Row 7: Attach black yarn. Ch 3, dc in each of next 3 st, *3 dc in ch-3 space (make stitches over rather than in chains to cover up pink), dc in each of next 5 dc*, repeat across with 4 dc in last ch-3 space, dc in last 4 st.
Row 8: Dc in each st and ch across.

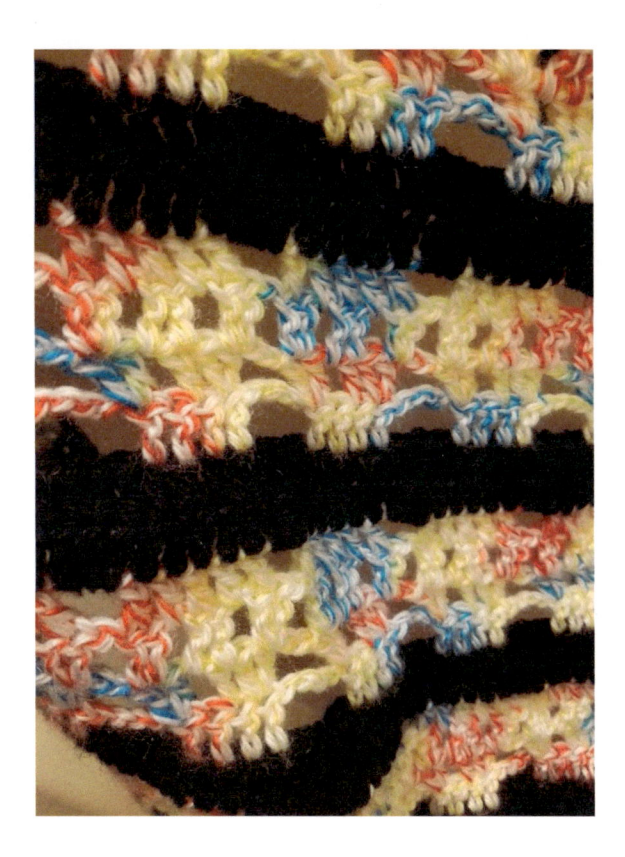

With right sides facing, sew short side of front to top of back on the left. Then sew short side of back to top of front.

Bottom edging:
With right side facing, attach black yarn to bottom edge and work 1 row of dc evenly spaced around the bottom with 3 dc in front and back corners. End off.
Top edging: Attach black yarn to top edge and work 1 row of dc around, decreasing at front and back corners. End off. Weave in all ends.

Fringe:
Cut 12" lengths of both colors of yarn. Using 3 pieces of the same color, fold in half and insert hook from back to front of bottom edging. Pull loop through stitch, then pull ends through loop you just made. Work 1 fringe every 2 stitches across bottom, alternating black and ombre.

CROCHET ABBREVIATIONS

bp	back post
ch	chain stitch
dc	double crochet
fp	front post
hdc	half double crochet
lp(s)	loop(s)
rnd(s)	round(s)
sc	single crochet
sl st	slip stitch
sp(s)	space(s)
st(s)	stitch(es)
tog	together
tr	treble crochet
yo	yarn over

My Fingers Fly

www.myfingersfly.com

www.myfingersfly.etsy.com

www.facebook.com/myfingersfly

@myfingersfly

@myfingersfly

amazon.com/author/lisaferrel

www.myfingersfly.blog

Member Of CGOA — Master of Advanced Crochet Stitches & Techniques
www.crochet.org/member/myfingersfly

Shop crochet patterns and fiber artist gifts at www.myfingersfly.com.

Feel free to share photos of your projects at www.instagram.com/myfingersfly or www.facebook.com/myfingersfly.

Follow My Fingers Fly blog for weekly tips and free patterns at www.myfingersfly.blog

Amazon Author Pages:

Crochet – https://www.amazon.com/-/e/B014TACPZO

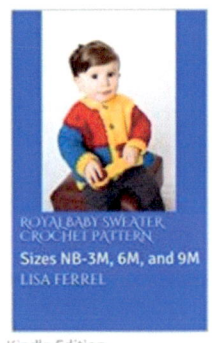

Poetry - https://www.amazon.com/-/e/B07QG6XYQP

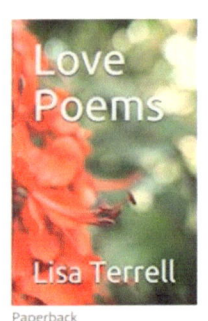

Made in the USA
Columbia, SC
05 April 2024